chroma.

© Copyright 2016 by Willie L. Kinard III
All rights reserved. Except in the case of brief quotations and questions embodied in critical articles and reviews, no part of this book may be reproduced in any manner whatsoever without permission from the author.

The selected poem herein previously appeared in the following publication: *For The Scribes*: "Elegy for Old Leaves"

A *For The Scribes*™ Collection
www.forthescribes.com

Printed in the United States of America
Book Design: Willie L. Kinard III
Second Edition

The ink scribbled on my wings
may fade as fast as their patter stops.

But, you will remember the colors,
you will remember the hum.

— *polychromatic breakdown.*

chroma.

POEMS BY
WILLIE L. KINARD III

A *For the Scribes* **COLLECTION**

On the bruises.
On the scars.
On the tears.
On the laughs.
On the relapses.
On the recovery.

On all the hues the prism emits.
On colorfulness.

Hues

Pink House Prophecy	8
Lit	10
Biscuits	12
Atlas Complex	14
Embers	16
Bruises	18
Sober	19
Gray Space	21
Insurance	23
Pollock	25
We Don't Cross Our Legs When Sitting	28
Constellations	28
Spin Cycle	30
Reliquary	32
To Ms. Effie White	33
Cusp	34
Bones	35
Staccato	36
Insert a Gas Station	38
Queen's Gambit	39
Tailwind	40
Butterbeer	41
Groomsmaids	44
Elegy for Old Leaves	46
Alchemy	47

Pink House Prophecy

Pink House be Refuge.
Traveler of forgotten promises left on the
doorsteps of Fourth Street, between stanzas be solace.
The pen an instrument of crafting lines even
the sober would snort, my therapist says I'm a masochist
for the highs of leaving it on a stage or a page. Be high.
Cloud nine. Shepherd of cirrus and cumulonimbus,
always with my staff and dope ass shawl.

Be Eros.
Love child of Siren and Minotaur,
stuck in like square pegs in round womb-bearers,
tell me what good is drawers-melting charm if
I'm bullheaded, strong-headed,
push up against those blessed rivers I part
with my lips whispering the hymns of
fallen soldiers' combat boots?
Like Noah, this rod be steady,
shepherd's staff be hooked,
be looking like snake,
be nook in cranny, be snake charmer,
be asthmatic, be bum rushed.
No, be bum lust, be box liquor,
be boxed wine, be boot bandit,
No, be boot knocker,
be knock, be knock, be knock,
they knock, they knock, they knock,
They steadily collide
and drip nectar into these chapters,
some never leaving these pages,
at least two be scratched out,
be formatted,
though one's ink be fresher,
still wet on my fingers.

Be Asylum.
My lyrics be needles, my fixes be stitched into
my tongue's tales, weaving elegant introductions,
adhered to the jolt of static pages revived
under moonlight, be born of lightning.
These botched pieces be rival to Shelley's beast,
be echoing Harris and Langston,
be students of Grimes and Draper,
of Bluford and Meyers,
be magic like Rowling,
be Bud of Curtis, not Buddy,
be Watsons, be Birmingham,
be eternal, be life, be breath,
be water, be fire, be butter, be biscuits,
be bread, be mead and mutton,
be torment 'till dew kisses
the dawn on its way to work,
be dew drops, be sunlight, be moon dust.

Be Destiny.
They say the men that came of this house so far
be no count, be washed out, be let downs.
They said be something.
Said be anything.
Be handy.
Be working, less talking.
Said be gentle.
Be nimble, but not quick.
Said be agile, be long run.
Be Godly. Be deadly.
Be serious. Be loose.
Said be more than.
Said be better,
simply better,
simply be better.

Working on it.

Lit

or For the Laid-back Folks that Have to Get Up,
Introduce, and Re-establish Themselves Just so
You Don't Get It Twisted

Historically, I'm known as one of the quiet ones,
but what's funny is that it is 2016,
and you still think we don't ever clap back,
so let me put you up on game right quick.
Don't fuck with me.

I am the perfect blend of my mother's temperance
and my father's temper, so if you mess with me, simpleton,
know that there are days that Mama doesn't
always win when my fuse is short.
I'm peaceful.

When common sense rarely decides to show up
and be present in your conversations, I'm good.
Otherwise, when even your own feeble prayers won't
offer you salvation from your lies and foolishness, I'm lit.
Like little flames to jumping jacks crackling over pavement
that you're too busy chasing in hopes of getting stacks,
I'm getting fed up with you niggas claiming you've got fire
when I've sneezed snot hotter than your rhymes on accident.
Boy, you need Poligrip 'cause your cool fell out when
your mouth fell down from being bitch-slapped by reality.
I'm nothing to play with.

Irrelevant ass.
Closed up tighter than a Mason glass jar,
You mad 'cause I erased your bars or 'cause you can't catch this?
Matchless. Matches to barns and sand to glasses,
let me hand your ass back that trash you came in my
face with like I'm supposed to be intimidated.
Boy, the Boogeyman can't be replicated 'cause I stopped

fearing him when I was four years old, bring warm to the cold,
head down, hustle like I'm solely here to do it again.
Reborn from ashes, never mind the dust,
don't look at the scratches, I'm a phoenix, boy,
coated in flames brighter than your shallow mind will ever be,
shining from the top of my head to sole of my feet.

On shining seas and purple mountains,
you will remember when you were astounded when
I rose from soot that no, you can't stick your cigarette in.
Like you, it's used up, has been, don't ever try again
to pollute my air with some mediocre shit in this room.
Boy, bye.

I have homicidal soliloquies written specifically
to put posing niggas like you in tombs,
scribbled eulogies on the backs of
bubble gum wrappers 'cause there ain't enough room,
it takes more than that to get me to move.

Fully reclined, I don't lose my cool,
smoking ain't my style, though I can spit like
dragons puffing shroom clouds.
Man, I don't need loud 'cause you already hear me,
so if you gone come at me, come harder than that.
Like it's your last night in Vegas and
the girl in the back of that cab says *Let's go*.
I'm gone already, rocked hard and steady,
and still going 'cause man, I don't chase shit no more,
'cause the flies already follow me and you can
promptly get to the end of that line.

Biscuits

Biscuits and the summer breeze,
floating through the house,
rolling in a small puddle of butter,
sizzling as it hits the side of the pan,
awaiting the few ounces of jelly, marmalade or jam
that'll be spread evenly on the split body of warmth
that I hold in my hands, trying not to let it
fall back on the plate, on the saucer,
in the state of being warm and delicious
that I didn't take care of properly,
that I dropped you see?

But, offered to me,
I hope will be your heart.
I hope will be your mind.
I hope will be your conversation and laughs every time that
I happen to say something funny that strikes a chord that
produces a delectable echo that bounces off of the walls
and the ceiling that gives me a feeling that you might
just be right for today, not tonight 'cause I'd like to be
a gentleman before that got started and way after that
but if you feel like that's where the night will go,
then we might not need to just yet,
that's a burden we ain't ready for yet, but know what?

If you're worth it, then I'm sure that the knife
and jelly that Mama gave me with the notes
Take care of the ones you share this with will be held steady
so that I may cut the bread and butter that you bring
to the table and if I'm able, it won't fall off of it onto the
bed of dirt below that somebody forgot to sweep
'cause he didn't wanna share in protecting a heart.

That's what possibly broke mine some time ago.
To be left in the dust, bathing in the ashes,

nothing to pick up but fragments of a shattered love
that I just couldn't seem to hold wholly again
without hurting myself, but I'm tired of hurting,
and I'm tired of feeling indifferent about things
that I once felt for you and I loved you.
I loved you like an alchy loves liquor.
You were so sweet and I was so drunk and so easy,
but that's saying something about me, ain't it?

But, do you think I give a damn?
Do you think that I really gave you up that easily?
Believe me, it took forever to get past you, but I'm through
with looking at reflections of fallacies that I know,
that God knows I know ain't even true, so before you even
get a chance to speak, don't interrupt my conversation again.

I apologize for my dissociative moments,
my flashbacks of being a resident of the Heartbreak Hotel,
but if I break bread with you, realize that I don't have
the prettiest plates to put it on, but I swear they're clean.
There are just some stains that you don't easily get rid of like
not feeling good enough to bring a new guest over for dinner,
or worrying that they'll laugh if you even mention
sopping jelly, but I'm finally feeling good enough,
I'm finally feeling ready 'cause I've swept up the crumbs
beneath the table and dusted the floor and mopped that thing
until it glowed and found some old candles and replaced
the broken screen door handle and I'd like for you to come over.

To share a bite, to shed some light on the gray subjects
that I haven't had the pleasure of putting gravy on yet,
of listening to the moisture that accompanies strawberry jam
falling on your napkin that you had to bib like a baby's
and watching you drop a bit of bread while you laugh.
And, while you fumble with the kerchief and stumble with
words in hopes of not offending me, please understand:
I could never be offended by a man that I want to eat a
biscuit with who knows to bring his own knife and butter.

Atlas Complex

The gods are petty.
Neptune makes maelstroms in his bathtub,
Persephone summers in paradise,
Zeus is a hoe, Hera punishes his conquests,
and I am burdened with the weight of
holding up an abandoned responsibility.
I am tired.

Thoughts of suicide left me black and purple with bruises,
but I pass them off as stains from partying with Dionysus,
and yes, that nigga turns the entire fuck up.
I've never had a hangover, but I've often
drowned my sorrows in tear-tinted wine.
I convince myself that I am alright, I am okay,
I am fine, I'm fine, I told you I'm fine.
I want my childhood back.

I want so much to be a carefree black boy again
whose daily motivation was gummies and Beetleborgs,
to feel the wind in my hair from the swing set or
blood rush to my face from hanging on monkey bars
and not from the screaming matches with Mama because
I don't know how to not be scared when we get home at night,
so stop making me an adult before my time.

I feel robbed. I feel cheated.
I feel like it's not fair.
I feel like I'm not supposed to complain because
1.) I'm still alive and
2.) it could be worse, but
3.) this isn't living.

To be a makeshift father-figure though all I want is
to be held by someone who doesn't live here anymore
so I learned to do it myself.

I don't know how to not be strong.
I don't know how to not be fearless.
I don't know how to be anything less
than a slow burn from Hephaestus so
yes, I get mad when even Plan Z doesn't go well.
Yes, I anger when I can't figure things out.
Yes, I know how to make due with what I don't have.
Yes, I learned it at too young an age.
Yes, Hell hath no fury like me enraged.
Yes, I shudder when that flicker goes out
and there's not a second wind left in me
to fuel it because all that has plagued me
is that I have one job—to not let it fall,
even when I don't feel like it anymore,
but I am tired of having to keep everyone
in mind at the expense of my feelings,
exhausted of taking care of people,
making sure that everyone else is alright,
when I'm left in ruins and being too proud
to admit even to people that love me
that I can't do it all by myself.
I hate it had to get to this point,
but there's no consequence in resting.

Hello, my name is Atlas.
I don't know how to let people do things
for me without returning the favor.
I am still learning how to ask for help,
that I don't have to explain myself,
that *No* is a complete sentence,
and that I don't have to carry
the world on my shoulders.

Bear with me.

Embers

There's supposed to be something noble
about extinguishing flames, right?
I'm no firefighter with some truck and sirens,
but I saw the smoke and thought I'd come
smother the fire anyway and that should
make me some sort of hero, right?
Eh... I didn't think so either.

Like honestly, you're probably looking at me
like who in the hell do I think I am,
showing up right before you dial 911 because
I had a feeling that you just might be in trouble?

A savior? No.
A psychic? Not really.
Presumptuous? Possibly, but can you blame a man
that doesn't care to see a house that he worked so hard
to build up burn down due to carelessness?

Love, that took time and the bricks and mortar laid
that embody that building, I refuse to let be emblazoned
on my corneas and in my memory as I hear you
scream from being singed by him—I can't allow it,
you see because the burns you have, they go down to
the white meat and you don't understand how much
cooling down I had to do to make that pain go away.

Mentally rolled it over, stopped and dropped it faster
than hot irons on my skin that, in turn, left scars on you,
temperatures of what exactly I'm not sure...
Countless degrees, 2nd or 3rd, or maybe 90 more,
but he still couldn't make it right if he tried.

He wasn't doing it right and you know it.
He didn't make you laugh like I did,

didn't know your fears like I do.
How many buckets have I poured on you
because he was too stupid to stop playing with matches?
I've dusted off so many damn ashes, but he keeps lighting shit
and I have a short fuse, so don't blame me when
I go off the next time because I told you...

Never mind.

I'll just wait, right?
Like always, he burns shit and I'm the first with
the salve to ease the pain, scrambling through rubble
and debris to find sooty remnants of what's left,
salvaging pieces that there ain't enough skin left to graft
and his laughter, selfishness and lack of consideration that
crackles behind the flames—that shit burns me the hell up.

I'd love to show him that hot coals ain't so therapeutic
and that these wisps, if you will, do more than
follow you through the forest, leading you to streetlights
on the avenue of Incandescent Ignorance—they'll hurt worse
than hot wax sealing promises of his future ass whipping,
but I think I know of a better use for these candles.

I'll show you that lighters ain't so bad in the right hands,
hands that'll light up more than your night,
but your life and don't burn to the touch,
touch much more, or better yet, touch me and my burns that
I got a while back from playing with fire but since then,
I've learned how to catch it, and mock me not,
I won't let it burn you and no, this isn't a game,
this is not a game, love;
it's just fiery.

And, I know you're hungry and cold
and I realize these flames look small
so let me help you fix your lips a bit
and join you in blowing on these embers
so that no one's left shivering in the dark.

Bruises

The purple spots are from the last one.
The reds ones, from the fights.
The tear stains, from the exit.
The duct tape, from the recovery.

I know you could easily undo it.

I hope that you don't.

Sober

I look at my hands and see the lines
etched into my palms that tell my fortune;
an inescapable predicament that says
at some point in time, I was bound to suffer,
but never did I think I would see the day
when my reflection scared me again.

I thought I was past that,
over the long-lost hatred
I once held for the face that
I met eye-to-eye in the mirror.

Bloodshot, dimly lit, hazier than vodka shots
that I don't have the patience to chase.
I want to feel everything and it's been
a minute since that corkscrew got used.
I need to feel alive, feel bees hum in my head,
'cause right now what I feel is pain.
I've been on Cloud Nine for a while.

Sir, rockets couldn't put me any more gone,
but if I'm being real, I think it was actually
Number Two or Three because honestly,
it ain't that peachy no more.

No matter how many times I put the bottle down,
I can't stop drinking my own words,
an acidic soliloquy wearing holes in me
as it escapes the fortress of my lips,
chucked with bitter backlash,
re-poisoning my ears, filtering nothing,
funneling down, *Too skinny, short as fuck,*
broke, balding, useless, ugly, weak.
I cringe and throw one back, 90 proof,
proof that this really ain't worth my dollar
but keep the change.

A penny for your thoughts, dime bag for tomorrow,
Bartender, give me some rum, as few rocks as you can manage.
No gravel or sand, but salt around the rim would be nice,
or instead give me a shot to fade from *I know why*
your dad ain't here. He didn't love you anyway.
Another for *You shouldn't have broken her heart,*
Two more for dismantling a happy home,
one for calling him back that night,
some gin for the heartache,
Jack for catching feelings,
Henny for not sleeping…

Just give me the damn bottle.

I said I wanted to get fucked up,
not fucked over, especially by this,
'cause I can't even remember when I started.

How many? I don't know.
Somewhere between buzzed and falling,
calling on Jesus and whomever else is listening
when the blue lights flicker, trying to get below 0.08,

but I'm 0.05 seconds away from throwing fingers
that say fuck your damn feelings and I'll be damned
if I stop 'cause I'm trying to drown them all
because I don't want to feel them.

But, I felt them this morning.

I ain't even lightweight, but I felt them this morning.
Didn't chase a damn thing, I felt them this morning,
Moaning to the bathroom only to regurgitate
fermented words that I knew only last night,
accompanied by bruises, the likes of,
I am very familiar with, but I ain't got time.
I'll save it for when Father comes looking for his money
back from Mother, but ain't nothing natural about the fight
I got into last night that I can't even remember,
but they tell me it ain't go well.

He looked like me, sucker punched me
with some shit I wasn't ready for,
did some damage to my head
and I can't even show the scars
'cause that's the second time.

Or is it the third?

Countless times, countless wounds,
pounded into the side of my head until I flinch
by the sheer thought of them and of him,
or rather he who stands on the other side
of my mirror saying he can't deal with this shit sober,
and threatens me that he won't or else.

But, do I hand him that corkscrew again?

Gray Space

Choose you this day whom ye will serve. (Joshua 24:15)

I met a woman with abandonment issues,
two kids, two baby daddies, shacking up with the latter,
claiming she'll never be alone that turns her nose up at
the women that stress themselves out, bending over
backwards to keep their no 'count men by their pillows.
She tells me she's holy.

You got it. Why you playing? Yo mama got it...
Mama broke her back and hurt her hips to make sure I got
through school after not being the first one out when
the death angel wanted to play dodge ball with my psyche.
Didn't have my first personal shower till I got to college,
so this art don't pay for itself, but it will soon, but it don't now
and I don't have the body to strip to pay my car note,
booty ain't big enough to be cruising the streets for
my next sugar daddy, so I don't know how to answer
Are you grown yet?

I fell in love with men that I thought would treat me like
the prince in the glass box, but ended up like the pauper
in the plastic one 'cause I'm a dented collector's item
torn from my priceless package without reading
the instructions for some immediate action.
Go figure, they didn't have to play with
me to tell me my love wasn't enough.

I stay up late having midnight conversations with the stars
and sometimes have a hard time making sense of
There are some things that we're not meant to understand.

End quote. Start thought. Don't question, why not?
Lot's salt, Ham's curse, Gomorrah's purse
or rather pocketbook had angels wanting it,

Jacob's wrestle, prism colors, more like prison colors.
Said *What you showing? How you eating?*
The G.O.A.T. gruff, always bleating, wood and nailing,
silver boy, ever rolling, ever sailing on waters troubled,
ain't got it to give it 'cause bridge tithe doubled
and trolls from the Southern Wild get paid no mind.

Told me I can't direct the choir no more.
Said *All that ain't necessary, you acting brand new.*
Said *You acting like your shit don't stank.*
You ain't even got coins in your bank
and you sweet so God don't want you.
Said *You done forgot where you came from,*
said *You acting like you been on son.*

No, I've been acting like I've been on one addiction
after another and finding a fix right now would be
all too satisfying for almost fitting the qualifications
of too many familiar disappointments.
So, I'm working to not hurt nobody
trying to figure out why this skin ain't worthy,
this voice too big, these embers too little,
these lashes too pretty to be my own,
these biscuits too burnt to be shared,
this body too impure to be a temple,
got more Greek in it than a Pentecostal Temple,
got more gray in it than on my mother's temples,
massaging my own to not say something unholy.
Said I'm unholy for just my thoughts,
bet dollars on bottom, descendant of Sodom,
said my five-year-old self chose to be
black and poor and proud and unfree,
said my inspirational R&B ain't gone be playing
from no space up in heaven so I need not apply.

My reply: If I'm waiting on your god to lie
and offer me circumstantial living arrangements,
let me get back to you on my decision.

Insurance

Officer, there is no reason that at twenty-two
I should already be at peace with death.

A collision incident at a traffic light that landed me at a corner
store one Friday morning that I openly admit was my fault,
shouldn't have me speaking aloud to calm myself down.

Before you approach, I make sure to make no sudden moves.
My wallet with jingling pennies will not
be mistaken for a gun today.

Another officer arrives not long followed by a state trooper,
and you say that this is standard routine as I'm swallowing
my nerves to be as polite as possible when I say I understand.
But, it's hard to rationalize why I'm wondering if my sisters
will be strong enough to sing at my homegoing, if my friend
in the passenger seat will remember the pass code that
I gave her to call if she's to be the bearer of bad news,
if my name will follow a hashtag before the sun sets this evening.

I am shaken as there is no coverage on whether my brown
body is insured by acts of the senseless,
only license to kill if deemed I was out of hand.

I step out of the car as the trooper instructs, call my mother
at his prompting to figure out which report should be filed,
when put on speakerphone for clarification from him,
I don't know if my nervous silence
was understood as a cry for *Help me.*
This is not the moment I need her
to be my concerned black mama.
I need her to be cooperative.

Crossbreed of black soap and Greek love,
I am five foot, six inches and 120 pounds of

still starry-eyed dreams and a large vocabulary,
armed with nothing but words of hemlock,
but I don't need proof to tell me that I'm not
already intimidating men twice my size;
they are ready to act with bullets of
the strongest anti-venom if either of us
draws our fangs.

Neon-colored Tasers taunting me on your hips that
I doubt would be used if she becomes belligerent,
I pray I'll see her later today.
I know by the elevations in her voice that
she can't see the three of you circled around me
or see the goodbyes that I whisper into the air.
I have no hair to be flung to the ground by
but I know that you're capable of bringing chicken,
soda and pound cake to my doorsteps and
wouldn't knock to be let in first so if I'm no longer
interested in the narrative that says *Not all cops*,
tell me why do you inflict fear in the people that
you're supposed to protect or is it a farce?

Officer, son of ebony darker than mine,
I don't mean to be rude when you imply that
you're a good one but the America I live in
won't let me forget that I'm a brown-eyed boy to
clutch your purse at, that this skin makes my
citizenship conditional, and that these stars and stripes
would strangle me until my blood salts this land of the free.
I am more worried about your peers.

You said that you don't like to screw people over.
My question to you is this: In that instance,
if shit went left at that gas station that Friday morning,
would my mother be picking out a tie for me this week?

Pollock

They say that masterpieces are artists' claims to being
recognized by society, a higher level of being noticed by
the upper crust, some Greenbacks for paying your dues,
as I adorned dew in the vastness of your courtyard,
once standing in the likeness of David,
I wonder if I get a dollar back for being witness to
acrylics and oils and watercolors that I'm not sure
I even want anymore.

My body is a canvas plagued and manipulated
with work that I'm struggling to call art right now,
but I'm afraid to show anyone because they'd see me
as nothing more than a graffiti-covered wall.
All I wanted was for you to love me, but the price came at
way too high a cost for me to go back to customer service,
asking for a refund, I run no more and neither do these colors.

They say patience is a virtue, but I've sat and received every
concept you could think of, each idea you could perceive,
watched you stretch me wide and thin across this easel
to points I didn't believe were possible, so forgive me
if I don't snap back the way I used to.
I guess I'm used to being left high and dry
when it mattered, tattered on the edges so much
that I was no longer appealing, revealing tears that
I didn't want you to see, but they're here so will you stay
and help me mend them or go find a new canvas?
Though I never felt like your boyfriend,
we were immortal.

We were immortal.
Marveled in marble, they stood in awe of us.
Wondered how they could get less flaws like us,
they'd ask us if we thought we were men or
the offspring of gods, but nod not we did, but laughed,

but chuckled at their foolishness as if we'd ever reveal
who we were to mere souls made mortal by their mortars
and pestles, crushing flower pistils and stamen into
sterile poisons that made stagnant their blood,
blood can't rush when hearts aren't pumping,
or when juice of Dionysus doesn't get hormones to jumping.
You can't kiss away the lumps in my throat that hold back
the bitterness I swallowed to become pristine again.
No Janet, no Michael, you won't make me scream again.
Man, it's not Wednesday anymore,
so can we find something else to do?

Can I not talk to you like I used to when we were
still friends, coloring inside the lines, trying hard to
impress each other like we knew what we were doing,
not getting high from the paint fumes, in your room,
finger-painting on funny textured paper, felt me, melt me,
melting wax to bronze until wax was no more,
acid bath in chemicals, my film revealed four,
or five or six or nine or seventeen or twenty-eight or
two and a half years worth of images I don't have sleeves for,
apple martinis until you were drunk, piss, pour it on me until
I no longer remember my original hues, call it a waste of time,
ask what did I love you for as if roses I painted for you
I didn't lose sleep for, or did I, did we not call on
the Fates to bring us our fortunes?

Funny 'cause when I met you, you loved one more,
but wouldn't let me go when I walked,
wouldn't let me speak when I talked,
wouldn't let me see another 'cause you wanted
me to yourself but didn't wanna care,
let you treat me like an option,
though I didn't wanna share you.

I had no place to feel like I did, but I wept.
Let you find in me a home, you crept over here,
scrubbing yourself in the morning, and making me a liar,
calling on my sister though she knew that I had lied to her,

cried to her, watched you call me ain't shit 'cause I had someone
else's signature, though I didn't belong to you in the first place,
expected me to change my status on the Book of Faces...
Face facts: no.

No.

Too much affection in public I don't like,
but I ain't trying though? You forget the third
monthiversary you made me remember,
but I can't get upset though?
No regrets though.
No regrets.

Said my anger had no warrants as if my love for you
didn't flow in torrents, downloaded knowledge on shit
I didn't even care for, gave you everything I had,
but you expected me to give more, heart torn,
black thorns on roses I would give to you,
but I ain't wasting 'em, holding on to inconvenience
but it ain't even chasing me, but it craved me,
leading me to darker places, trying to run in hopeless races
while erasing the words etched on my skin for you,
holding my face together for *But I love him too.*

You'd ride, I'd ride. You'd ride, I'd ride.
You'd ride, I'd ride, you'd ride, I'd ride, you know
I died too many times for you, in too many cases.
Baby, I love you, but I have no more empty space on this
canvas for you to throw paint at and call me your masterpiece.
I am not your Pollock so you will not drip drops on me
and expect me to dry and hang with it.

We Don't Cross Our Legs When Sitting

I have no interest in
throwing my crown off balance.
Queen Clarisse taught me better.
Neatly, at the ankles, dear.

Constellations

When you returned,
I had all intentions of taunting you
and leaving until we embraced.
I forgot what it felt like to be hugged.
Wow. It's been a while.

Moonlit benches after sidewalks and rounds of
Crown and cranberry seemed sobering,
though we both knew that the gods were watching
and we were far from caring.

Though not drunk in love, we were enjoying
the shot of a moment, laying all cares to the wind,
bathing underneath meteor showers and
distant streetlights buzzing in and out of existence.
Speaking in forbidden tongues that were only
audible when caressing earth tones,
my feet walked amongst the divine tonight
and Gemini may have soul for it,
but I don't care.

I watched the heavens bachata tonight,
joined David and his fellow Goliaths on the floor,

danced right out of my clothes, will probably blame Venus
for it in the morning, though Mercury will say otherwise,
and maybe there's chips of satellites in my mustache,
maybe there's moon juice on my lips, grass stains on my socks,
stardust in my skin, and no breath left to kiss you with,
but we made love under Cygnus and Andromeda tonight.

I counted just as many stars in
your eyes as I found in the night sky.
Your black plane dipped in the oceans of my planet
and you drank till your beard had been watered,
filled your cup till it ran over, scattering drips in
craters of mine before they hit elsewhere.
I wished on that shooting star, knowing not
of what I spoke to that comet, just remembering
how vast the Milky Way was and how no one
can hear you scream in space, but reciting chorus of
Cosmic Journey in keys of the Fifth Element.
This be no Hadley Street Dream birthed,
but the release of a rapture long awaited for.

Apocalypse devoured everything, but onto your board,
you silver-tongued surfer, you cradled me.
Maybe there is more to you than I thought.

When I wake up, there will probably be
traces of space debris at the corners of my eyes.
I will replay the scenes of where star trails
danced along our bodies countless times over.
I will find frozen spoons left in orbit too long
to cover the spots of impact, will blush and deny
all accusations of interplanetary exploration,
only strengthening the light of the corona around me,
and I will smile, looking to the sky and
trace your face amongst the constellations.

I don't know what you freed tonight, but thank you.
I needed that.

Spin Cycle
Spots Left Over after the Wash

I hope that I didn't capture too much
of your laugh when our souls last exchanged
because he might mistake it for mine the next time
my giggle becomes a guffaw topped with elaborate gasps
dripped over it that don't belong to me anymore.
And though dripping droplets are the last of my worries,
I'd be a fool to say that every now and then I'm not still stung.
That wound didn't heal completely before I took the bandage off.

I am trying to be gentle with myself,
but I don't have the best blueprints to go by.
I haven't been handled with care in a long time,
so my fragile sticker falls off from my shaking
when he reaches to touch my face because
the words that have left welts on it were
much more dangerous than his hands.

I wasn't ready.
Not for the end of it, not for the bitterness, not for the
daydreams, though they should be called morning tremors,
because they fucked up my mood worse than two
tequila sunrises before dawn; I still feel sick sometimes.
I still feel dirt behind my ears, I still feel like I'm looking
over my shoulder, I still find traces of you in my eyes or
my smile or the wrinkle above my brow because
I don't want to remember the bad because
I'd have to admit where that furrow came from.

We weren't twins. We weren't copies of each other,
but every thing in me says that I've known you
in a past life and that doesn't lie, makes no mistakes,
so avoiding a certainty instilled in you can be
understood as self-care.

Where the spirit leads, go.
When the spirit says, leave.
What the spirit cries, write.
Her tears wash truths from feet too
soiled to put through the spin cycle.
I have walked in muddied territory so much
that I have to triple check to make sure that
it wasn't me who left footprints on the new carpet.
I bought a rug to cover the holes that were burned in the floor
and covers for the arms of the chair that he still wants to sit in,
prop his feet up reclining, and I'm honestly surprised.
He says there's some cosmetic damage, but what good one
hasn't had at least one who didn't think so before he let it go?

I thought I let it go, I thought I had to run,
I thought I had to make nice with you to gain peace again,
but I'm not offering two fingers any more or *Fuck you* fingers
any more, not tumbling down my dash gazing at
relationship goals of Bey and Jay, we might be me and bae soon,
but I am owning every color that came of this wash that
you didn't care to separate darks from so you get no more
instructional tags, I am leaving your bags and boxes by
my back door so you can get them whenever.
This is the last time I'll tell you.

I hope that I didn't capture too much
of your laugh when our souls last exchanged
because he might mistake it for mine,
though maybe, another go might get that out.

But, even if it doesn't,
if bleach doesn't work,
if I can't scrub any more of you out of me,
the good thing is that so far,
he doesn't mind the little spots
and still likes me when I'm fading.

Reliquary

When I found God, I did find not Him slinking
beneath the pews, waiting to start an erratic lap around
the sanctuary, whilst I carefully rattled the wrapper from
my peppermint between the spurts of the power tap theme.

When I chose prayer, I did not choose it on some altar,
on my knees before a vessel too crooked to be anyone's
holy man proclaiming that everything I wanted would
be answered if I surrendered to the force that required
my first tenth that I could not see.

When I caught the Spirit, I did not catch it as the choir
soared during the 2nd key change, there was nothing holy
stirring up inside me as I dodged the bells of a flailing
tambourine set on fire by the middle member of this trinity.

I caught it in my bathroom, dancing and stomping
and two-stepping beyond belief saying,
I don't have to be hurt by them anymore,
with the speed and precision of a monk,
revealing the battle scars of love's last stand, with burns dark
enough to see and stretch marks large enough to be proud of.

I chose it after the breakdown in my car, after the grieving by
my bed post, after the gay didn't go away, but my virginity did
with him, when I refused to be nailed and bloodied to
this rainbow, when I gave up my cross to bear witness to
an energy housed here that hell shivers under
and even my healing stones tremble at.

I found Her when turning the knife over in my hand and seeing
the inkling of a power and a brilliance mirrored in its blade,
rattling to the shake of my shoulders and Mama's voice breaking,
reflected in my bloodshot eyes, mouthing the words,
You are not finished yet.

To Ms. Effie White

You were our sister and I know you said Curtis was perfect,
but if this is the best that you've come in contact with,
how many ogres and trolls have you made yourself smaller for?
For how many dawns did you compromise your time?
Just how many men have you had attach muzzles on
your mouth hoping to extinguish the flame,
made you wonder if your own name
was that of a tarnished angel?
Honey, how did you withstand them all?

Like big brass and smitten saxophones, you sang like
your landlord backstage needed the late fee and all you
could shake out of your boots were rusty nickels.
Golden-throated brown woman, my queer self found more of me
in you in two hours than in many of these past years of mine,
I've never been the one center-staged for a him either.

You were a dream, a morning tremor worth waking up for,
a woman scorned with redemption on her lips,
a change in her song and an attitude not up for negotiation;
I know what it's like to squeeze your voice thinner,
to hide behind something common for so long that when
you started lagging behind he never noticed the difference.
You remind me that we've all got pain and
that it's okay to feel winded sometimes.

I carry your melodies in my back pocket for rainy days
as reminders that if my being a little big-voiced,
brown boy is a bondage, I don't wanna be free.
All I know how to do is sing these lines I write at 3 a.m.
and tell my reflection that one day this will all be worth it.
Effie, you taught me this:
If he ever tells you you're doing too much,
never compromise your magic
because heavy ain't for everybody.

WILLIE L. KINARD III • 33

Cusp

I wrote about you today.
I always heard that if you weren't written about,
it wasn't important, that whatever happened
didn't mean anything, that almosts don't count,
but I think, I think that I didn't want
to write of you out of wrath.

I don't remember you as bad.
Just young.
You were young.
I was too.

Impatient, but trusting.
Both still figuring out how to move in the dark,
how to move with borrowed hearts and flashlights.

You were the first time something felt right,
that I felt right, that something real, that I felt loved.
You were love, but also labor, but I stayed, forgave you,
and I held your hand and I lay on your chest,
and I laughed and I listened to your fears.
It seems like a dream now.

I'll never forget you lying your head in
my lap crying, you were tormented.
I felt broken, like faulty wiring,
like damaged goods, like trampled heartstrings,
split between what wasn't, what was,
what had been, and what was to be.
Or, rather what could be.

You were balance, you were grounding,
you were reminders that love is
everything you can give honestly
and that almosts still matter.

34 • CHROMA

I miss your hugs and your lips.
I miss your hands, strong, curious and gentle.
I miss your smile, warm and hearty.
I still think about you.
I'm proud of you.

There are no hard feelings.
You taught me things.

I am worthy of being loved.
I got my heart back.

I wrote about you today.
It was important.

Bones

While drying steam's tears before
my noon-thirty shadow dance,
the boy in the mirror has stepped out of the shower.
Autumn breath his towel, I double take.

Honey cashew colored, thin thigh meeting narrow hip,
shoulders defiantly broad, nipple free, arch.

Body tightly wrapped around clavicle and jawline,
he stares at mine as if it's familiar,
following high metabolism and
wisps of musculature intensely,
with eagle accuracy.

He smiles.
I wink.

Staccato

For someone that's really good with words, you'd think
that I wouldn't be such a klutz with them around you,
that I wouldn't stumble over my own tongue so much,
that I could flip a coin into the mouth of your fountain
without dropping it, but my brain can't make heads
or tails of any of those magnificent gifts of yours,
I am spellbound and wondering where you've been all of my life.

You are haven.
You are lighthouse.
You are warm cabin.
You are oil to creaky door hinge.
You are earmuffs to screechy chalkboards.
You are lake frozen over to winter boots that
don't have to worry about falling or sinking anymore,
I can skate for a bit.

I've always loved the warmth of these hills.
Water runs from the mountain almost instantly
at the sunrise of your smile, no longer dripping in incessant
staccato, but flowing until everything is leaking and growing.
Ground is firm here, there is green here, enough to
get high as hell off of, I am standing at the peak of this
anti-molehill dizzy from the airwaves, befuddled from
lack of oxygen, only wanting to return the echo
of your voice that bounces of these walls.
These mounds are asylum, this ground is bedlam
and moans of this wind tie me in a straitjacket,
Your rhythms leave me questioning my sanity
in dazed ecstasy and still, I am yet sane.

Maybe it's the scorpion's opus that I'm hearing,
suffering from venom that I don't want the antidote to,
I just want to be buried underneath mounds
housing a spring that quenches an insatiable thirst,

maybe it's wanting to lick every drop of poison from
your exoskeleton with your legs wrapped around me
taunting me with your tail, maybe it's being myself with you,
that my spirit now runs in tandem with yours,
maybe just a third below, that I have found a
rhythm to keep up with, that I've imitated your timbre,
that I know every note in your scale, that I haven't been right
since I gave you my sheet music, you made it your own and
you're only one I ever want to hear play it again.

Make music with me,
give me reason to learn every
flourish and riff in your ornamentation,
let me soar to the optional note in your descant.
I will come to those heights and will sing every pitch in
your legato line on *Uh* and *Mmm* because there is nothing
more satisfying than hearing you gasp at finding out
just what you've been practicing your deep breathing for.
I am flatfoot, knees bent, shoulders back, stomach relaxed,
jaw dropped, belting this beautiful rhapsody you've composed.

You don't know what you do to me.
I don't have to stutter anymore.

Insert a Gas Station

The eleventh minute
brought no penny candy
or brown paper bag.
No milk for the parlor.
No cream for the kittens' bowls,
They've scratched up your chair leg.
The little one has stopped
curling up in the seat.
He doesn't like it cold.

It was when you left that I wanted
to bundle up in your arms and
tell you to take me with you.
I couldn't tell you that I wanted to be
everywhere that wasn't where I was,
I couldn't tell you that I'd miss you
and that I felt deeper things than
this *enjoy each other's company.*

You were everything that I didn't need
but were all the things that floated
that I loved when you picked me up.

Like balloons.
Like there was hope for us.

That was over a month ago.
The empty bottles are still by the door.
I left the light on.
You said it'd only take ten.
I'm not sure if
I should still be waiting.

Queen's Gambit
To D4

I never thought that our Saturday morning brunch
would turn into a spades game.
What was supposed to be checkers,
requiring no heavy lifting, soon became
world-class chess heavy and me trying not to show my partner
just what I was feeling when I was down on my luck.
Lucky me that I found my need to retire early was
accepted as not trying hard enough to put up a fight.
Who knew you'd come out swinging when
I told you I'd leave the gloves at home?
Such a classic opening.
I guess that chest shot was my fault.

I let you move me like a pawn,
only forward by your decisions,
never being able to go back,
to retrace my steps, to fall down, to retreat.
Only forward, only one step,
always controlled, always predetermined;
my fate is not to be rescued at your discretion.
Though I am smaller than you, I be no damsel, but you
damn sure be that knight that will always move 3 spaces.
Though you got to third base, baby, that *L* you form
you should soon get used to, Sire.

Or, should I call you Bishop, Sir Holier-Than-Thou?
There be no hell you can put me in without sitting
there with me, no heathen label you can stick on my chest,
no *F* as scarlet letter you try to sew on me thinking
I'm afraid to fail, like I give God no glory upon new dawns,
though I praise Him for keeping my pulse steady,
my temper cool, my hands away from clubs.
These clubs be the resting place of weak hearts attracted

to diamonds hours away that dismiss and attempt
to destroy the holy that resides in these coverings.

Boy, my Sabbath be this word,
commune when parchment meets this pen.
This paper be the body,
this ink be the blood and
you should thank Him for experiencing
the ghost that be this ride and grind.
I heard you still call out for it.

To think, I castled you, My Liege.
To think I covered you only for you to renege for no reason.
But, those jesters be talking, those jacks be quick,
and boy, I might be a queen, but what's a king
that can only see movement inside his own box
to a Queen that has the whole board
to his disposal to prance around?

Tailwind

I have not been here before.
I lay caution to the wayside,
riding this tempest until it peters out
accepting wherever it dumps its sand,
I am not lost.

I have not been here before,
but I am throwing Mercury's logic to the side,
spelunking with no map,
no knowledge, just feeling;
I am not lost.
I have not been here before,
but during my solar return,

I am distant from Virgo,
for a second, to feel gravity,
instinct, charm and all,
with a Libra's heart.

Maybe these scales will
balance out in our favor.
Perhaps, one side,
we will both sit in.

I am not lost,
but I am finding something.

Butterbeer

Word to Dean Thomas for surviving until
the end and making this venture easier.
Respect to Hermione Granger, though you'll
always be a black girl with a fro in my mind,
thank you for making books magical and necessary.
And, respect to Albus Dumbledore, for being so
but never letting them forget that you were
the baddest muhfucka to ever don a purple cloak.

I think the sun broke through the clouds today.
After sifting through yestermonth's dirty laundry and
failing to be able to get my umbrella up in time to avoid
the damage of the downpour, the rain has finally stopped.

There are feathers in the air from swallows
being the Whomping Willow's latest victims,
the selkies are murmuring in the lake
just below the surface, the squirrels are scampering
through the grounds, in hopes of shedding their

chicken nugget bellies and I am almost home.
There is a barbecue with my name on it,
a shot to be taken in my honor and
the days are steadily disappearing.

I am finding myself wrapped in the fading ink of
job applications, sealed with the hot wax of hope,
I consult the main line so much that I wonder
if God hesitates to answer when the caller ID reads
Bald Brown-Eyed Man with a Dream.
I have dreams of one day moving
audiences of hundreds with my lines,
though even just one with my rhymes is humbling.
I'm fumbling in my speech trying to articulate my thoughts,
but my words don't fall to the ground anymore.
I have ground coffee and milk running through my pores,
my skin radiates a drunken bliss that you can't
buy at the liquor store, I'm finding my art to be
intoxicating again just when I needed it to be
and it is breathtaking.

It is painstaking to perfect the art of not being sarcastic.
It is earthshaking to love yourself even when you feel static.
It is news-breaking to be built of something
sturdier when everyone else seems plastic.
It is hard to reflect on four years of magic and
expect yourself to sum it up in just one poem,
but to the people that I owe my growth to,
I think that it is worth a try.

To brothers that remind you that you still ain't shit,
but support you every step of the way,
and mothers that wake at 5 a.m.
just to see if you're okay,
it took everything in me not to break down when
you hugged me on Sunday, but I think I'll be alright.

To sisters that hold you down and will run up
on niggas that think that they might have

any sort of ideas about getting in your face,
a mug to you all, I raise.

A glass to friends that brought their own knife and jelly,
that hold you in the middle of the night when
everything shatters and help you pick back up
the pieces when you thought you'd never find them.
When you see how much of them are inside you that
you didn't see yourself inside them too,
I wonder if I would've made it without you.

To ex-lovers whose arms I found comfort in:
when the lesson has been learned,
when all anger has faded,
love is all that remains
in this cup for you.
I wish you well.

So here's to butterbeer at Hogsmeade
after reunion shows and road trips,
to broken curses and turning more pages,
to leaving more of it all on stages,
to new adventures and better beginnings.

Finite.

Groomsmaids
Dear Future Husband

Weddings scare me.
I am twenty-two, the words *I do* leave a bad taste
in my mouth and in the past few years,
too many people I know have crossed off
getting hitched before 30 as a major goal of life.
I am not one of them.

I enjoy my space, get nervous in front of new company
and large amounts of people drain me really quickly.
I'd rather drink at home and have really stimulating
conversations with the select few folks that I call friends
that are more like extended family.

To varying extents, we all are hopeless romantics that
either sing or write poems about love and navigating
the troubled waters of modern-day relationships,
secretly hoping that the perfect bridge will show up
and save us from the shit-lists of our pasts.
I often wonder what my own wedding will be like.

I envision it'll be simple and small,
elegant with pairings of colors like viridian and
white peach and tasteful arrangements of type
that I took months on deciding on each of
the invitations and the favors for our wedding party.

As you guessed there will be no brides here, but while
beautiful music permeates the air like the sweetest of perfumes,
my side will be sure to have a few groomsmaids two-stepping
down some aisle ahead of me, ready to bear witness to a feat
that I'm sure we all thought would never happen, but they're
intent to seeing for themselves so dear Future Husband,
I hope you're ready to always be under intense scrutiny,

to be examined like a tsetse fly under a microscope carrying
malaria that could kill me with the slightest bit of bit contact.
My brothers are trained-to-go to rip you to pieces
at the drop of the first tear you cause.
Please proceed with caution, I beg you.

Dear Future Husband, I hope you're ready to deal with
some mood swings that baby, even I can't prepare you for.
Just pray that androgen cycles, full moons and
Mercury Retrograde don't happen at the same time.
I will need tissues, lots of hugs, and even more sex.
God bless you; you've been warned.

Dear Future Husband, I hope you're ready for some of the
most intense caring and support that you've ever fathomed.
I am small in stature, but giantesque in my loving and
I dare a nigga to ever attempt to hurt what is mine.

That being said, dear Future Husband, do not make me mad.
My best friend has planned to escort you out prior to detonation.
My bark is bigger than my bite, but I've been known
to destroy walls and pride with the most cutthroat of words,
leaving only debris and bruised egos in the wake of my echo.
Like a sleeping lion, I spare no one once provoked.
Don't tempt me with this bachelor party.

Dear Future Husband, I am stubborn,
nerdy, take too damn long to get dressed,
harmonize the background vocals of anything that
comes on the radio, can be calmed down with an apple,
already have names for our children, love Skittles
and scalp massages and express myself way better
in writing than I ever could aloud so if it looks like
I'm no longer trembling while I'm saying my vows,
you can believe that either grabbing your hands stopped
my nervous shiver with the warmth of shared eternity
or that I wrote them down first.

Elegy for Old Leaves

Bootleg bass lines over late night breezes, September is a tease.
Flirting with the equinox and lay-over for 80-degree weather,
Virgo season foreshadows a homegoing.

A funeral of heat, a cremation of daylight,
a spreading of ashes on tax-free weekends,
and a reminder that Darkness remembers that
Dusk is his mistress during the year's last quarter,
no matter how much she cries for him in May,
her voice only stronger in October.

Taking green from matured saplings,
dropping like blowflies after insecticide,
they remind me of the fallen leaves of my family tree
and how any sign of color is always short-lived,
always ridiculed and chastised, scorched.

Great-grandmother's voice took power from burns.
I wonder how much warmth she left us
to eulogize summers with.

Such a beautiful death, to go out in color.
To go out, in color, adored. To go out, in style.
To go out, like skin shed. To go out, like old leaves.

I have imitated these leaves, disappearing under ice.
But birth, but glorious rebirth.

Spring always follows with instruction.
Nurture. Hydrate. Prune. Defend.
Soak in this light.

I garden this bed,
rake out old leaves,
expecting fruit.

Alchemy

I stopped sweeping the shards of broken flasks
when I realized Mr. Flamel was oblivious.
Hair more silver than his brass would ever be,
he snickers and tells me genius is color-coded,
importance is expensive and my coins don't
add up enough to be pausing his search,
so I have no business meddling
in alchemy if I can't afford it.

So I wonder if Peter keeps a record on me.
News of his frequent robberies are becoming
more and more widespread and by now,
I would think that he and Paul would've realized
that their signatures were on each other's receipts.

I don't have a lot of money.
Just two quarters in my pocket to rub together
that tell me I still have too much month at the end of
my paycheck and while I am trying to melt down
their powdered wigs into something more permanent,
Flamel never mentioned to see myself as a living treasury,
worth more than a circumstance.
Though I know I am heir to many frequent sailing miles,
he looked for a fountain in my people's homeland,
but rid it of its supply of immortality.

A breathing earth, I am personified platinum and ebony,
gold dust springs from my skin under sunlight.
I am 24-carat mutable coconut and hibiscus, ask me
the last time I transformed into something unstoppable,
I'll say it was this morning.

Unmatched and I don't need to wave my hand over
any brew to become something more prominent,
I am already here.

Wax print patterns knitted on my bag of
essence of palm ash and shea butter,
I am descendant of healers and elders that
would break chicken bones over grease fires,
humming and moaning whispers of well-being,
prosperity and safety into my future.

I am broke, but unbroken;
bent, but unyielding;
reasonably supple, but headstrong;
aging, but forever youthful and envied;
brown target, but carefree and formidable.
I am black boy magic.

Nicholas, what you were looking for
was right under your nose the whole time.
Your elixir lives here.

Milton Keynes UK
Ingram Content Group UK Ltd.
UKHW041348191124
2962UKWH00016B/75